My Life, My Story

A Mother's Legacy Journal

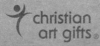
christian
art gifts®

My Life, My Story...A Mother's Legacy Journal

© 2012 Christian Art Gifts, RSA

Christian Art Gifts Inc., IL, USA

© 2012 Meadow's Edge Group LLC

Scripture quotations in this book are taken from the *Holy Bible,* New Living Translation, first edition, copyright © 1996. Used by permission of Tyndale House Publishers Inc., Carol Stream, IL 60188. All rights reserved.

Editorial development by Todd Hafer

Designed by Thinkpen Design LLC

Printed in China

ISBN 978-1-4321-0181-7

Contents

Introduction

Every mother has a story. It is time for me to share mine.

In my life, I have learned so many things about what is truly important, including the love, laughter, and legacies that families share and pass on from generation to generation.

As life moves along, memories become one's constant companions, but they can also be gifts—gifts meant to be shared with those you love. Gifts that celebrate the enduring bonds of family.

As I share my life with you in these pages, I will pass on the wisdom, values, and memories that have graced my days— with the hope that, somehow, reading my story will help you write yours, beautifully and meaningfully.

With Love,

_____

Me: At a Glance

"Before you were conceived, I wanted you.
Before you were born, I loved you.
Before you were here an hour, I would die for you.
This is the miracle of life."

MAUREEN HAWKINS

I will wait for the LORD . . .
I will put my hope in Him.
I and the children
the LORD has given me. . . .

ISAIAH 8:17-18

Here is the story of the where and when of my birth . . .

_____

_____

My full given name is . . .

_____

_____

My name was chosen by . . .

_____

_____

I was given this name because . . .

_____

_____

The first nickname I can remember was . . .

_____

_____

I earned this nickname because . . .

_____

_____

My mom's full name and place of birth are . . .

_____

_____

My dad's full name and place of birth are . . .

_____

_____

As for siblings and their birthplaces . . .

_____

_____

_____

_____

_____

_____

_____

_____

_____

_____

_____

My maternal grandparents are . . .

My paternal grandparents are . . .

My husband's full name and place of birth are . . .

As for my children and their birthplaces . . .

A Few of My Favorite Things

"True, a mother has many cares.
But they are sweet cares."

JULIETTE MONTAGUE COOK

Your heavenly Father already knows all your needs.
Seek the Kingdom of God above all else, and live
righteously, and He will give you everything you need.
So don't worry about tomorrow.

MATTHEW 6:32–34

My favorite way to spend a day is . . .

_____

_____

_____

_____

_____

As a child, my favorite TV show was . . .

_____

But now, my favorite is . . .

_____

If there is one movie I can watch over and over, it's . . .

_____

I love this movie because . . .

_____

_____

_____

_____

_____

_____

My favorite sport is . . .

_____

I like this sport best because . . .

_____

_____

_____

My favorite team is . . .

_____

My favorite athlete is . . .

_____

My all-time favorite vacation place is . . .

_____

I love vacationing here because . . .

_____

If I could eat only one food for the rest of my life, it would be . . .

_____

My "guilty pleasure" when it comes to food is . . .

_____

_____

My all-time favorite song is . . .

_____

_____

Here's what makes this song special to me:

_____

_____

_____

_____

_____

_____

_____

_____

_____

_____

_____

_____

_____

My favorite activity is . . .

_____

_____

This activity is tops because . . .

_____

_____

_____

_____

_____

_____

_____

_____

_____

_____

_____

_____

_____

A perfect night out for me would have to include . . .

_____

_____

_____

_____

_____

_____

_____

_____

_____

_____

_____

_____

_____

_____

_____

The skill I'm most proud of is . . .

_____

_____

_____

_____

_____

_____

_____

I first knew I had this ability when . . .

_____

_____

_____

_____

_____

_____

_____

_____

People tell me my best trait is . . .

In *my* opinion, my best trait is . . .

If I could change anything about myself, it would probably be . . .

A typical day for me is sure to include . . .

My Life as a Little Girl

There is a garden in every childhood,
an enchanted place where colors are brighter,
the air is softer, and the morning more fragrant than ever again.

ELIZABETH LAWRENCE

You made all the delicate, inner parts of my body
and knit me together in my mother's womb.
Thank You for making me so wonderfully complex!
Your workmanship is marvelous—how well I know it.

PSALMS 139:13-14

Here's what I remember most about my childhood home . . .

_____

_____

_____

_____

_____

_____

_____

When I recall my bedroom, here's the picture that comes to mind . . .

_____

_____

_____

_____

_____

_____

_____

_____

_____

_____

If you could walk through my old neighborhood, here's what you'd see:

_____

_____

_____

_____

_____

_____

_____

That neighborhood is different today, because . . .

_____

_____

_____

_____

_____

_____

_____

_____

_____

My childhood best friend was . . .

_____

_____

_____

_____

_____

_____

_____

We got along because . . .

_____

_____

_____

_____

_____

_____

_____

_____

_____

As a child, my favorite thing to do was . . .

_____

_____

_____

_____

_____

_____

_____

My *least* favorite thing, on the other hand, was . . .

_____

_____

_____

_____

_____

_____

_____

_____

If I was a child prodigy at anything, it was . . .

_____

_____

_____

_____

_____

_____

_____

My fondest wish as a kid was . . .

_____

_____

_____

_____

_____

_____

_____

_____

_____

My favorite childhood toy was . . .

_____

_____

_____

My favorite book was . . .

_____

_____

_____

Back then, my favorite place to be was . . .

_____

_____

_____

I loved that place because . . .

_____

_____

_____

_____

_____

If you were looking for me and my friends, you'd most likely find us . . .

As for my religious foundation and childhood memories of church . . .

The scent that always takes me back to my childhood is . . .

My most treasured childhood memory is . . .

The childhood experience that influenced me most was the time . . .

My Family Life

"Every child born into the world
is a new thought of God.
An ever-fresh and radiant possibility."

Kate Douglas Wiggin

Direct your children onto the right path,
and when they are older, they will not leave it.

PROVERBS 22:6

When my mom was younger, she looked like . . .

_____

_____

_____

_____

_____

_____

_____

If you entered our house, you'd most likely find my mom . . .

_____

_____

_____

_____

_____

_____

_____

_____

_____

When my dad was younger, he looked like . . .

If my dad had a catchphrase back in those days, it would probably be . . .

As best as I can remember, my mom spent her days . . .

My favorite thing to do with my dad was . . .

I'm like my dad because . . .

_____

_____

_____

_____

_____

_____

_____

But Dad and I are different when it comes to . . .

_____

_____

_____

_____

_____

_____

_____

_____

_____

_____

It's hard to believe that my dad used to . . .

_____

_____

_____

_____

_____

_____

_____

If my mom had a catchphrase back in those days, it would probably be . . .

_____

_____

_____

_____

_____

_____

_____

_____

_____

When I was a child, my dad's occupation was . . .

_____

_____

_____

_____

_____

_____

My opinion of Dad's job was . . .

_____

_____

_____

_____

_____

_____

_____

_____

As a child, my favorite family activity was . . .

_____

_____

_____

_____

_____

_____

_____

My favorite childhood memory of my mom is . . .

_____

_____

_____

_____

_____

_____

_____

_____

_____

I'm like my mom because . . .

_____

_____

_____

_____

_____

_____

I'm different from my mom because . . .

_____

_____

_____

_____

_____

_____

_____

_____

The best way to describe our economic status back then would be . . .

As for household responsibilities, my parents insisted that I always . . .

My parents encouraged me by . . .

A couple of my all-time favorite family memories are . . .

When it came to getting along with my family members, I was . . .

As for childhood pets, my favorite was . . .

Here's what I miss most about being a child . . .

My earliest memories of grandparents are . . .

My favorite memories of visiting my grandparents, or their visits to me, are . . .

Here's what I loved most about my grandparents . . .

_____

_____

_____

_____

_____

_____

_____

_____

One valuable lesson I learned from my grandfather or grandmother is . . .

_____

_____

_____

_____

_____

_____

_____

What I know or remember about my *great-grandparents* is . . .

Some things I know about my family history and my ancestors are . . .

The aunts, uncles, and/or cousins I have been closest to are . . .

_____

_____

_____

_____

_____

_____

_____

_____

_____

_____

_____

_____

_____

_____

_____

_____

_____

_____

At family reunions, I . . .

_____

_____

_____

_____

_____

_____

_____

The strangest relative I've ever met was . . .

_____

_____

_____

_____

_____

_____

_____

_____

My favorite home-cooked meal was . . .

_____

_____

_____

_____

_____

_____

_____

The snacks and special treats I remember my family enjoying together were . . .

_____

_____

_____

_____

_____

_____

_____

_____

_____

When my family had company, I . . .

_____

_____

_____

_____

My favorite place to eat when my family dined out was . . .

_____

_____

_____

_____

Here's why I loved that place . . .

_____

_____

_____

_____

_____

When I was a child, weekends were . . .

_____

_____

_____

_____

_____

_____

_____

On family summer outings, we usually . . .

_____

_____

_____

_____

_____

_____

_____

_____

_____

During the winter, my family and I liked to . . .

When I think of my family, the first words that come to mind are . . .

My Education

"Knowledge is the power that gives us wings to soar."

ANONYMOUS

Those who search will surely find me.

PROVERBS 8:17

I attended elementary school at . . .

_____

_____

_____

_____

_____

_____

_____

My earliest memory of school is . . .

_____

_____

_____

_____

_____

_____

_____

_____

_____

In elementary school, the things I enjoyed most were . . .

_____

_____

_____

_____

_____

_____

_____

The things I enjoyed *least* were . . .

_____

_____

_____

_____

_____

_____

_____

_____

I attended middle school at . . .

_____

_____

_____

_____

_____

I attended high school at . . .

_____

_____

_____

_____

_____

My all-time favorite school subject was . . .

_____

_____

_____

_____

_____

_____

My favorite extracurricular activities were . . .

_____

_____

_____

_____

_____

_____

_____

_____

A memorable award I received in school was . . .

_____

_____

_____

_____

_____

_____

_____

_____

_____

My memories of my favorite teacher are . . .

Some of the fashion trends during my school days were . . .

In my yearbook's senior-class photo, I look like . . .

Some popular songs I remember are . . .

_____

_____

_____

_____

Some movies I remember seeing include . . .

_____

_____

_____

Some television shows I enjoyed are . . .

_____

_____

_____

_____

When I was a teenager, the big celebrities were . . .

_____

_____

_____

_____

Some things I remember about learning to drive are . . .

_____

_____

_____

_____

_____

_____

_____

My first car was . . .

_____

_____

_____

_____

_____

_____

_____

_____

At dances and/or parties, I usually . . .

_____

_____

_____

_____

_____

_____

_____

The biggest challenge of my teen years was . . .

_____

_____

_____

_____

_____

_____

_____

_____

If I had to re-live my high school years, this time I would . . .

During high school, my goals and aspirations were . . .

After graduating from high school, I decided to . . .

I am so glad I did *not* decide to . . .

When I moved away from home, I . . .

_____

_____

_____

_____

_____

_____

_____

My first dorm room or apartment was . . .

_____

_____

_____

_____

_____

_____

_____

_____

_____

My favorite memories of college are . . .

_____

_____

_____

_____

_____

_____

_____

Today, my connection to college is . . .

_____

_____

_____

_____

_____

_____

_____

_____

_____

Me: On the Job

"A mother could perform the jobs
of several air-traffic controllers with ease."

Lisa Alther

*Work willingly at whatever you do,
as though you were working
for the Lord rather than people.*

COLOSSIANS 3:23

When I was growing up, I wanted to be . . .

_____

_____

_____

_____

_____

_____

_____

My first job was . . .

_____

_____

_____

_____

_____

_____

_____

_____

_____

My first *career-oriented* job was . . .

_____

_____

_____

_____

_____

_____

_____

When I first got this job, I felt . . .

_____

_____

_____

_____

_____

_____

_____

_____

_____

The things I liked about this job were . . .

_____

_____

_____

_____

_____

_____

_____

The most enjoyable job I ever had was . . .

_____

_____

_____

_____

_____

_____

_____

_____

The worst job I ever had was . . .

The most memorable place my work has taken me is . . .

A co-worker or boss who was a valuable mentor to me was . . .

An experience I had in mentoring someone else was . . .

Some valuable friendships I gained through my work were . . .

The most important things I've learned about life through my career . . .

_____

_____

_____

_____

_____

_____

_____

_____

_____

_____

_____

_____

_____

_____

_____

My Love Story

"Alone we can do so little;
together we can do so much."

HELEN KELLER

Two people are better off than one,
for they can help each other succeed.

ECCLESIASTES 4:9

My first crush was . . .

I attended my first boy/girl party when . . .

Here's what I recall about my first kiss . . .

Here's what I remember most about my first date . . .

A typical teen date usually included . . .

My first true love was . . .

I met my spouse when . . .

_____

_____

_____

_____

_____

_____

_____

My first impression of him was . . .

_____

_____

_____

_____

_____

_____

_____

_____

_____

The qualities I admired most in my future husband were . . .

_____

_____

_____

_____

_____

_____

_____

As we got to know each other better, I learned . . .

_____

_____

_____

_____

_____

_____

_____

_____

_____

The length of our courtship was . . .

_____

_____

_____

_____

_____

_____

Our favorite date-night activity was . . .

_____

_____

_____

_____

_____

_____

_____

_____

I knew I had found "the one" when . . .

Here's what was most memorable about the marriage proposal:

Our wedding took place . . .

_____

_____

_____

_____

_____

I wore . . .

_____

_____

_____

_____

My spouse wore . . .

_____

_____

_____

_____

_____

A few of the most-special guests included . . .

_____

_____

_____

_____

_____

Our "first dance" song was . . .

_____

_____

_____

_____

My fondest memory of my wedding day is . . .

_____

_____

_____

_____

_____

For the honeymoon, we went to . . .

Right after getting married, we lived . . .

A typical evening during my early years of marriage was usually . . .

I first began thinking about having children when . . .

My closest friends from those early marriage years were . . .

The leisure activities I came to enjoy in married life were . . .

To me, here is what is most rewarding about marriage:

To maintain a healthy marriage, I think it is important to . . .

A time in my marriage when I learned the true value of teamwork was . . .

_____

_____

_____

_____

_____

_____

_____

_____

_____

_____

_____

_____

_____

_____

Today, here's what I value most about married life:

My Life as a Parent

"We find a delight in the beauty
and happiness of children that makes
the heart too big for the body."

RALPH WALDO EMERSON

Seek His will in all you do, and
He will show you which path to take.

PROVERBS 3:6

When I first learned I was going to become a parent, I . . .

On the day my first child was born, I felt . . .

The significance behind my children's names is . . .

Having a newborn at home changes your daily life because . . .

_____

_____

_____

_____

_____

_____

_____

_____

_____

_____

_____

_____

_____

_____

_____

_____

_____

_____

Becoming a parent changed my outlook on life by . . .

My fondest memory from my early years of motherhood is . . .

The most fun a mom and dad can have with a young kid or two is . . .

When my spouse and I needed child-free entertainment, we . . .

My children are similar to me because . . .

_____

_____

_____

_____

_____

_____

_____

My children are different because . . .

_____

_____

_____

_____

_____

_____

_____

_____

_____

The most important values a mom can pass on to her child are . . .

My greatest joy in being a parent has been . . .

_____

_____

_____

_____

_____

_____

_____

My greatest challenge has been . . .

_____

_____

_____

_____

_____

_____

_____

_____

_____

My children's upbringing was similar to mine because . . .

_____

_____

_____

_____

_____

_____

It was different from mine because . . .

_____

_____

_____

_____

_____

_____

_____

_____

_____

Something I know now that I *wish* I had known in early parenthood is . . .

The thing I truly hope my children have learned from me is . . .

The most important thing *I* have learned from my children is . . .

A Life Worth Celebrating

"If you want a happy family,
if you want a holy family,
give your hearts to love."

MOTHER TERESA

Sing a new song to the LORD,
for He has done wonderful deeds.
His right hand has won a mighty victory;
His holy arm has shown His saving power!

PSALMS 98:1

When I was young, my birthdays were usually . . .

_____

_____

_____

_____

_____

_____

_____

My favorite birthday memory would have to be . . .

_____

_____

_____

_____

_____

_____

_____

_____

_____

My all-time favorite birthday present was . . .

_____

_____

_____

A special meal or dessert I liked to have on my birthday was . . .

_____

_____

The first holiday gathering I hosted was . . .

_____

_____

_____

If I were to grade myself on this event, I'd receive a (n) . . .

_____

_____

_____

My all-time favorite Christmas carol is . . .

_____

_____

_____

Christmas is special to me because . . .

When I was a child, Christmas was usually . . .

_____

_____

_____

_____

_____

_____

_____

_____

_____

_____

_____

_____

_____

_____

_____

_____

_____

A childhood Christmas memory that really stands out for me is . . .

A childhood Christmas tradition I have passed on to my family is . . .

The most meaningful Christmas for me as a parent was . . .

Things I will always thank God for . . .

When I was a child, my favourite holiday was . . .

_____

_____

_____

_____

_____

_____

_____

And a favorite summertime memory is . . .

_____

_____

_____

_____

_____

_____

_____

_____

As a child, Valentine's Day usually meant . . .

My Life: The Main Events

"Life is not measured by the number of breaths we take,
but by the moments that take our breath away."

ERICA FRANDSEN

Anything is possible if a person believes.

MARK 9:23

The happiest time of my life has been . . .

_____

_____

_____

_____

_____

_____

_____

The saddest has been . . .

_____

_____

_____

_____

_____

_____

_____

_____

_____

The busiest time of my life has been . . .

_____

_____

_____

_____

_____

_____

The most relaxed and carefree has been . . .

_____

_____

_____

_____

_____

_____

_____

_____

One event that really shaped my life was . . .

A political event that made a strong impression on me was . . .

So far, my life's proudest accomplishment has been . . .

An accident, major surgery, or prolonged illness I had to endure was . . .

A really difficult time endured by someone close to me was . . .

When I think of a tragic time in my life, I remember when . . .

The toughest decision I've ever had to make was . . .

My most memorable travel experience has been . . .

The first time I traveled by airplane was . . .

The farthest I've ever traveled from home is . . .

The most memorable place I've ever visited is . . .

Placing my faith in God has been a major event in my life . . .

A cause to which I have dedicated myself is . . .

My favorite competitive activity is definitely . . .

The award or honor I am most proud of is . . .

The most important invention of my lifetime has been . . .

The first time I helped someone in need was . . .

The scientific discovery that has changed my life most has been . . .

Since my childhood, here is how society has changed most:

One thing I would never change about the way I live life is . . .

One thing I wish I had done differently is . . .

My hopes for the world in the next 10 years are . . .

My hopes for me and my family in the next 10 years are . . .

My Sources of Inspiration

"Hold tenderly to that which you cherish."

Bob Albert

The eyes of the Lord watch over those who do right,
and His ears are open to their prayers.

1 Peter 3:12

The people who have made the biggest impact on my life are . . .

As a young person, when I needed guidance, I usually went to . . .

My faith in God has shaped my life . . .

A Scripture passage that has been meaningful in my life is . . .

If I could keep one family photo, it would be . . .

My most treasured material possession is . . .

_____

_____

_____

_____

_____

_____

_____

_____

_____

_____

_____

_____

_____

_____

_____

I still get a lump in my throat whenever . . .

I know that my life's ultimate calling is . . .

When I was young, my role models were . . .

_____

_____

_____

_____

_____

_____

_____

One famous person I truly admire is . . .

_____

_____

_____

_____

_____

_____

_____

_____

_____

A public speaker I enjoyed hearing (or would like to hear) is . . .

The author or book that has most inspired me is . . .

Other ways that I find inspirational moments in my day include . . .

Notes & Memories

*Don't copy the behavior and customs of this world, but let God
transform you into a new person by changing the way you think.*
ROMANS 12:2

We know that God causes everything to work together for the good
of those who love God and are called according to His purpose for them.
ROMANS 8:28

*You keep track of all my sorrows. You have collected all my tears
in Your bottle. You have recorded each one in Your book.*

PSALMS 56:8

Don't worry about anything; instead, pray about everything.
Tell God what you need, and thank Him for all He has done.

PHILIPPIANS 4:6

_Feed the hungry, and help those in trouble. Then your light will shine out
from the darkness, and the darkness around you will be as bright as noon._
ISAIAH 58:10